This book is dedicated to the fine art of living superbly and indulgently in the heart of the wild African bush. So while monumental New York thunders around you, take a moment and leaf through these exquisite bush camps of Southern Africa, and dream of wilder things. And then know that after a good shoot with us, we will take you there – after a great African shoot there is nothing quite like a wild bush night to wrap it all up.

Skysweeper Films produces and facilitates great commercial productions in Southern Africa. Come inside our vast playground and we will take you on a sophisticated ride ensuring a unique experience of our wild game, sand, sea and sun.

come inside with us…

Tel: +2711 460 1111
E-mail: titus@icon.co.za
www.skysweeperfilms.co.za

SIMPLY

SAFARI

FOR FRED AND MO/DAD AND MOM,

WHOSE LOVE AND SUPPORT HAS MEANT SO MUCH OVER THE YEARS

SIMPLY

SAFARI

DARYL & SHARNA BALFOUR

DESIGN BY PETAL PALMER

CONTENTS

CONTENTS

INTRODUCTION

SAFARI IS A SIMPLE SWAHILI WORD meaning 'journey', or 'to travel', but has come to mean so very much more. Imbued with a sense of the exotic, more typically a sense of Africa, the word safari has today become symbolic of something far more romantic; it evokes images of adventure and stylish indulgence as portrayed by actors Meryl Streep and Robert Redford in the 1985 film version of Karen Blixsen's *Out of Africa*.

'Safari' had, in fact, been adopted by the colonial elite who settled much of southern and east Africa more than a hundred years ago. Even Denis Finch Hatton, the legendary 'White Hunter' portrayed by Redford and who promised his clients spacious walk-in tents with high ceilings, crisp bedlinen and fresh laundry daily, piping-hot baths and ice-cold cocktails with fresh canapes, followed by dinner at an immaculate table set with crystal and silverware and accompanied by vintage wines, was following traditions set long before. Perhaps the first person to establish the idea of safari for the sake of simple pleasure and enjoyment – rather than adventure and hardship in search of fortune – was the 19th-century naturalist and British colonial army officer Captain William Cornwallis Harris. In 1836 he led an expedition through southern Africa whose sole purpose was to observe and record (by painting) the wildlife and landscapes witnessed by the expedition members. Schooled by the high style of the army mess in India, Harris ensured that his entourage did not suffer too many deprivations, though he did establish the safari routine still followed today – rise at first light for tea and a hearty breakfast, an energetic day in the wilderness with a midday nap under a shady tree, followed by a return to camp in the evening for a lavish dinner accompanied by fine wines before retiring to the fireside for cigars, port and tales of safari exploits. Later that century Sir Randolph Churchill (Winston's father) took this example even further while undertaking a lavish safari in what was then Rhodesia. His party was accompanied by a huge contingent of staff and lackeys and a wagon train loaded with what he considered to be the essentials – not only tents, beds, tables and chairs but also a full-sized piano, cases of whiskey, gin and wine, and crates of vintage champagne. Today's safaris are little different, though the establishment of permanent tented camps and lodges have negated the need for hundreds of porters, wagons and the like (though there are still any number of professional mobile safari operators who offer a taste of these expeditions of old). Nowadays Africa still attracts travellers with an adventurous bent wanting to experience wilderness in the style of some of those early explorers and naturalists, and they are able to do so simply by making a reservation at one of the operations catering to these needs. By perpetuating the traditions of these old safaris, adopting the decorative style and borrowing from early architecture, modern camps and lodges are able to offer a highly romanticised way of 'roughing it' and an experience

of great luxury and sensuality. In compiling this book we endeavoured to portray a cross-section of architectural and decorative styles, from the more traditional to the most modern, and from those built in original tented safari style to others that are more like small luxury hotels in the wild. In each of the southern African states we visited – Botswana, Mozambique, Namibia, South Africa, Swaziland, Zambia and, briefly because of the political turbulence, Zimbabwe – we saw diverse themes in design and decor, connected by threads of colonial grandeur tied with an African simplicity in a style that was quite simply, safari!

JACI'S SAFARI LODGE

madikwe game reserve
south africa

LEFT: ZIMBABWEAN STEEL

PANGOLINS OFFSET BY A

MALAGASY RAFFIA CLOTH

ADORN A HANDCRAFTED

POPLAR-BOUGH DINING SUITE.

ABOVE: A COPPER-AND-

BRASS FLUE ENHANCES

THE COSY WARMTH OF THE

SUNKEN FIRE PIT.

Open-plan lounges with blazing log fires, dinner under a ceiling of stars, and unique stone, thatch and canvas bedrooms create a safari ambience that melds perfectly with the charms of Herman Charles Bosman country. Nestled under a grove of tamboeti trees on the banks of the Marico River, Jaci's Safari Lodge pampers the soul with its blend of raw textures, natural fabrics, five-star service and gourmet meals. Drawing their inspiration from nature, owner-designers Jaci and Jan van Heteren have created a harmonious balance between the cosseting comfort of luxurious accommodation and the essential impression of being at one with nature.

Jaci's is situated within the recently proclaimed Madikwe Game Reserve, less than four hours' drive from Johannesburg.

ABOVE: CAST COPPER FROGS ADORN SIMPLE GARDEN TAPS IN A VERDIGRIS FINISH. THE BASINS IN THE BATHROOM ARE BEATEN COPPER.

RIGHT: THE SIMPLE WOODEN BED OFFERS THE ULTIMATE ROMANTIC EXPERIENCE WITH ITS EMBROIDERED WHITE COTTON COVERS, SILK CUSHIONS AND BOLSTERS. GAUZY MOSQUITO NETTING IS SUSPENDED FROM A WOOD FRAME HUNG FROM THE RAFTERS.

TOP LEFT: NATURAL LOCAL STONE HAS BEEN USED THROUGHOUT THE LODGE; HERE IT COMBINES WITH

LEADWOOD BEAMS TO FRAME THE CENTRAL HEARTH IN JACI'S MAIN LOUNGE. DEEP-RED WALLS CREATE

A WARM AND INVITING ATMOSPHERE THAT TEMPTS YOU TO RELAX INTO THE SOFT CHAIRS AND COUCHES.

BELOW LEFT: THE ART DECO LINES OF A SIXTIES JUKEBOX CONTRAST WITH THE STAINED CANE COUCH

AND COFFEE TABLE ACCESSORISED WITH WOVEN BASKETS AND COLOURFUL HAND-EMBROIDERED CUSHIONS.

A BEDU DANCE MASK FROM GHANA AND CARVED BATONKA DOORS FROM ZIMBABWE ADORN THE WALLS.

ABOVE: OVERSIZED CUSHIONS SCATTERED ON A GUDZA MAT — HANDWOVEN FROM THE BARK OF BAOBAB

AND MOPANE TREES AND TINTED WITH NATURAL DYES AND PIGMENTS — MAKES FOR A COSY BEDROOM CORNER

IN FRONT OF A CERAMIC FIREPLACE. IT'S THE PERFECT SPOT TO UNWIND WITH A BOOK AND BOTTLE OF GOOD

WINE AT THE END OF THE AFRICAN DAY.

MALA MALA GAME RESERVE

sabi sand wildtuin
south africa

LEFT: THANKS TO THE FORESIGHT OF MALA MALA'S FOUNDERS, THIS LEOPARD CUB HAS A SAFE HOME TODAY.

ABOVE: THE HISTORIC FACADE OF KIRKMAN'S CAMP STANDS AS A MEMORIAL TO ONE OF THE RESERVE'S PIONEERS.

Mala Mala is synonymous with southern African safari style and set the standards which others followed — combining uncompromisingly high levels of comfort, style and class with a superb wildlife experience. Today's owners, Mike and Norma Rattray, have kept the three lodges — Main, Harry's and Kirkman's — as vivid monuments to the reserve's pioneers. The atmosphere reflects Mala Mala's history as an area first preserved as the hunting retreat of early landowners, as the decor makes liberal use of mounted trophies, game skins and similar memorabilia. While this historic theme, encompassing the pioneering days of this region, runs throughout the three lodges, each differs in style and ambience in order to create a unique feel without losing that inimitable Mala Mala touch.

The decor at Harry's Camp is a testament to the spirit of the Ndzundza clan of the Ndebele people who live close to Mala Mala — their creative traditions of wall painting and elaborate beadwork have been a part of southern African culture for centuries. Meals served under the stars in this colourful fireside boma offer diners an added dimension to the excitement of the safari experience.

Hunting memorabilia and game trophies, historic black-and-white photographs and numbered wildlife prints by artist Keith Joubert create a clubby feeling in the Buffalo Bar of Mala Mala's Main Camp, where guests can gather for pre-dinner drinks to discuss the day's viewings. The bar, furnishings and wall panels were made from ancient kiaat (Transvaal teak) taken from trees that died on the property almost a century ago.

ABOVE: COLOURFUL NDEBELE DOLLS SET AGAINST A WOVEN WALLHANGING DEPICTING EARLY SAN ROCK ART, THE INTRICATE DESIGNWORK OF ZULU BASKETRY, THE TAWNY PELT OF A ROGUE LEOPARD, AND EARTHY ANIMAL PRINT CUSHIONS ON WICKER CHAIRS CREATE AN ETHNIC AFRICAN FEELING THROUGHOUT MALA MALA'S THREE LODGES.

OPPOSITE: A COLLECTION OF OLD BOTTLES UNEARTHED ON THE KIRKMAN'S PROPERTY IS DISPLAYED ON A WOODEN DRESSER, PART OF THE ORIGINAL FURNISHINGS OF THE HOMESTEAD DATING TO THE EARLY 20TH CENTURY.

LEFT: A HIGH THATCHED ROOF AND LIGHT-COLOURED WALLS AND BEDLINEN ADD TO THE SPACIOUS AND AIRY FEELING OF THIS BEDROOM AT MAIN CAMP. A BRIGHTLY WOVEN WALLHANGING KEEPS THE FEELING ESSENTIALLY AFRICAN.

ABOVE: A CUSTOM-MADE BUTLER'S TRAY MAKES A SUITABLE COFFEE TABLE IN THIS MAIN CAMP LOUNGE, WHICH IS REDOLENT OF THE TRADITIONS OF HUNTING LODGES OF OLD. SKINS AND HEADS ADORNING THE WALLS ARE OFFSET BY THE MUTED ORANGE AND RED MALI-WEAVE FABRIC USED TO COVER CHAIRS AND SOFAS.

SINGITA PRIVATE GAME RESERVE

sabi sand wildtuin
south africa

LEFT: TWO LIMEWASHED
BEDS PUSHED TOGETHER FORM
THE CENTRAL FEATURE OF THIS
CONTEMPORARY BEDROOM AT
BOULDERS LODGE, WHILE THE
USE OF MALI MUDCLOTH TO
COVER THE BOLSTERS ADDS
AN AFRICAN DIMENSION.

ABOVE: THATCH, UNTREATED
LOG UPRIGHTS AND EARTHY
WALLS AT EBONY LODGE.

Natural building materials such as locally garnered rocks, dark African ebony and tawny thatch help the lavish Singita lodges — Ebony and Boulders — retain an African simplicity despite their reputation for offering the last word in First World comfort. Ebony Lodge speaks of the traditions, art and culture of Africa with soft, comforting and luxurious finishes, while Boulders has a more contemporary feel, combining modern fabrics and finishes with traditional earthy tones and tapestries. Whether huddled over a steaming morning coffee or savouring sundowners on the deck overlooking the plains, at Singita you'll listen for the sounds of the bushveld while world-class comfort and style stroke the senses. Both intimate lodges offer private suites with their own lounge and fireplace, deck and plunge pool.

RIGHT: COMFY ARMCHAIRS INVITE RELAXATION ON THE PRIVATE DECK FRONTING EACH EBONY LODGE SUITE.

BELOW: WHITE LINEN SLIP-COVERS COMPLEMENT THE RICHNESS OF BROWN LEATHER CUSHIONS AND THE EARTHY TONES OF MALI MUDCLOTH.

BOTTOM: A BATHROOM IN BURNT ORANGE, RAW SLATE AND BRIGHT WHITE.

RIGHT: THE SOLID SILVER CANDELABRA IS BY ZIMBABWEAN SCULPTOR PATRICK MAVROS

AND THE WOVEN TELEPHONE-WIRE PLACEMATS ARE FROM ZULULAND'S SIYANDA WEAVERS.

TOP: THE EBONY LOUNGE INSPIRES A MORE COLONIAL ATMOSPHERE WITH ITS BLEND

OF WOOD, RATTAN, LEATHER AND ZEBRA SKIN, AND STRIPED AND FLORAL FABRICS.

BOTTOM: MURALS IN EBONY'S DININGROOM ARE REMINISCENT OF SAFARIS GONE BY.

LEOPARD HILLS GAME RESERVE

sabi sand wildtuin
south africa

LEFT: HANDCARVED WOOD INLAYS IN THE RECEPTION FLOOR DEPICT THE LEOPARDS AFTER WHICH THE LODGE IS NAMED.

ABOVE: EACH SUITE HAS SUPERB VIEWS OF THE SURROUNDING BUSHVELD.

Modern and stylish, Leopard Hills manages to combine hi-tech with the earthy feel of the African bushveld. Glass-fronted air-conditioned suites keep the summer heat out, while the use of tree-trunk pillars and archways, reed cladding and exposed thatch, khaki walls and coir matting creates a decor that is unashamedly luxurious without being ostentatious. Fabrics used throughout the lodge are a blend of savanna hues and neutral shades mixed with bold animal prints that create a peaceful environment in which to relax after an early morning game drive. A small lodge accommodating only 10 pampered guests at a time, Leopard Hills embraces a casual, family-style atmosphere with dinner served at a large communal table under the glittering canopy of the African night skies.

TOP: NATURAL LIGHT POURS IN TO ENHANCE THE SUCCESSFUL MIX OF TONES AND TEXTURES.

ABOVE: ROMANTIC GLASS-FRONTED BATHROOMS OVERLOOK THE SURROUNDING SAVANNA.

RIGHT: ORIGINAL VICTORIAN ANIMAL PRINTS AND A KUDU-HORN CHANDELIER WITH OSTRICH-EGG

SHADES VIE FOR ATTENTION IN THE WARM LODGE LOUNGE.

VUYATELA: DJUMA GAME RESERVE

sabi sand wildtuin
south africa

LEFT: BOLD USE OF COLOUR GIVES THE LIBRARY AND COMPUTER ROOM AN UP-TO-DATE MODERN LOOK.

ABOVE: A VENDA CRAFTS-WOMAN FINGER-PAINTED THESE WALLS USING BUFFALO DUNG.

Contemporary rather than classic-colonial. That's the feel of Vuyatela, where modern meets timeless Africa in a bright and colourful mix of today's township arts and crafts – using recycled materials – with cultural traditions and techniques. Galvanised iron combines happily with more traditional rock and mud-packing wall-building techniques, while untreated timber, thatch and finger-painted walls give the lodge its African vibe. Hand-crafts from nearby village communities grace the lodge walls and tables, alongside both classic and naive artifacts, historic documents and old black-and-white photographs. Vuyatela's proprietors want their guests to leave with a sense of the magic of Africa, embracing both the old and the new, the eternal nature of the wilderness within modern society.

THE MIX OF COLOURFUL TOWNSHIP ART, TRIBAL MASKS AND CALABASH BOWLS ON THE WALLS BLENDS WITH THE MORRIS

CHAIRS COVERED IN TANNED KUDU HIDE AND BUILT-IN SOFAS UPHOLSTERED IN NATURAL CHENILLE. THE 3-D ARTWORKS

ON THE LEFT ARE BY WELL-KNOWN CAPE TOWN ARTISTS JACKSON NKUMANDA AND LEON ZUMANA; THEY USE

RECYCLED MATERIALS SUCH AS CARDBOARD PACKAGING AND THE RUBBER SOLES OF DISCARDED TRACK AND TENNIS

SHOES. THE CERAMIC FIGURINES AND KITCHEN BASICS WERE HANDCRAFTED BY VICTOR MPOPO.

AN UNUSUAL CHANDELIER MADE WITH OLD COCA-COLA BOTTLES MAKES A STRIKING FEATURE ABOVE

THE DINING TABLE, WHILE OTHER LOCAL ART FEATURES PROMINENTLY THROUGHOUT THE LODGE. THE

PAINTINGS (TOP) ARE BY GHANAIAN ARTIST BLANCHARD ADAMS, WHO NOW LIVES IN JOHANNESBURG.

LEFT: THE BREAKFAST TABLE IS BRIGHT WITH REED AND SWEET-WRAPPER PLACEMATS AND BEADED CONDIMENT SETS PRODUCED IN A LOCAL SHANGAAN VILLAGE; THE HANDPAINTED NAPKINS ARE FROM THE PHILANE FLAGSHIP WOMEN'S GROUP IN CAPE TOWN.

TOP: THE GEOMETRIC DESIGN OF THE WOVEN RUG ENHANCES THE CHEERFUL TONES OF THE LOUNGE'S UNUSUAL BUT SUCCESSFUL MIX OF COLOURS.

ABOVE: HANDPAINTED CUSHIONS, A TRADING-STORE BLANKET AND GAILY COLOURED PAINTINGS.

SELATI LODGE: SABI SABI

sabi sand wildtuin
south africa

Selati Lodge, the flagship of the renowned Sabi Sabi Private Game Reserve, evokes the romance and nostalgia of a bygone era with its blend of steam railroad memorabilia, period furnishings and the deliberate exclusion of electricity. Lit at night by the flicker of oil lamps and lanterns, the lodge's romantically furnished and decorated suites hark back to the early 1900s. The lodge has its origins as a water and food stopover on the old Selati railway line that linked the Boer republics with the port of Lourenco Marques. Much of this history is reflected in the artifacts that decorate the rooms today, while many of the suites carry the names of stations and stops on the long-discontinued line. Rich textures, natural fibres and neutral tones combine to create a mellow tenor that makes one pause for reflection.

LEFT: THE SELATI LODGE AT SABI SABI IS NOTED FOR ITS RELAXED LEOPARDS.

ABOVE: A SENSE OF A BYGONE ERA PREVAILS IN THIS BEDROOM IN THE LAVISH IVORY SUITE.

THE MIX OF COLONIAL FABRICS AND FURNISHINGS IN THE LOUNGE CREATES AN INFORMAL AND RELAXING MOOD THAT IS

ENHANCED BY THE HISTORIC RAILROAD MEMORABILIA AND EARLY 20TH-CENTURY ARTWORK LINING THE WALLS.

ARTIFACTS FROM ANOTHER AGE, INCLUDING STEAMTRAIN NAMEPLATES AND SERIAL NUMBERS, COLOURED GLASSWARE,

SILVER COFFEE POTS AND A TREADLE SEWING MACHINE INDUCE A NOSTALGIC AIR THROUGHOUT SELATI LODGE.

ABOVE: OLD LEATHER SUITCASES AND A HATBOX

LEND AN OLD-WORLD AURA TO A CORNER OF THIS

ROMANTIC HONEYMOON SUITE.

RIGHT: A ZEBRA-SKIN RUG ON TINTED CEMENT

FLOORS AND MOSQUITO NETTING DRAPES ABOVE

THE SOLID TEAK DOUBLE BED LEND A DREAMY

FLAVOUR TO OTHERWISE SIMPLE DECOR.

LEFT: COPPER PANS AND KITCHEN UTENSILS HANG FROM THE CEILING AND EARTH-COLOURED WALLS OF THE COSY FARMHOUSE KITCHEN, CONTRASTING WITH THE SUMPTUOUS SILVER TABLE SETTINGS ON A SIMPLE GREEN-AND-WHITE CHECKED CLOTH.

ABOVE: OIL LAMPS SET A ROMANTIC MOOD IN THE IVORY SUITE BATHROOM. THE SENSE OF LUXURY IS ENHANCED BY THE PLUSH CHAISE LONGUE AND ORIENTAL RUG.

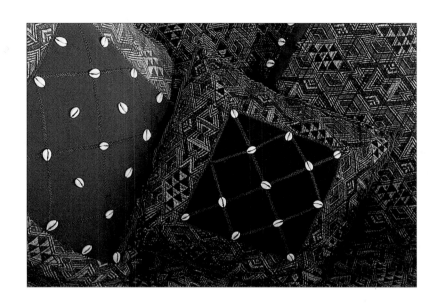

ULUSABA ROCK LODGE

sabi sand wildtuin
south africa

LEFT: Comfortable easy

chairs and kelim-covered

couches are the gracious

furnishings in this

spacious lounge and bar.

ABOVE: A rich blend

of textures and tones.

Sir Richard Branson, the new owner of Ulusaba Private Game Reserve, has spared no expense in turning his flagship Rock Lodge into one of Africa's finest game lodges. With each room decorated in a unique African theme and the lounge-dining area furnished in what can best be described as 'bushveld baroque', he has created a mountain eyrie of luxury and sophistication. Set atop the highest mountain *kopje* in the Sabi Sand, the lodge enjoys a spectacular outlook over the surrounding bushveld. Local artist Harem created several murals featuring tribespeople in traditional costume. The decor features original African artifacts, weaving and beadwork, seamlessly interwoven with rock, thatch, reeds and fine woods without compromising comfort, luxury or style.

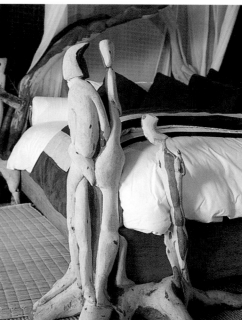

THE DECOR IN EACH ROOM

IS INSPIRED BY DIFFERENT

AFRICAN CULTURES, SUCH AS

MAASAI, NDEBELE, SAN AND

SWAZI. WALLS ARE COVERED

WITH VIBRANT COLOURS,

BARK STRIPS OR REED MAT-

TING TO CREATE A UNIQUE

AND INTRIGUING CHARACTER.

Traditional reed wall cladding combines well with natural coir matting in this warm Zulu Room. Clay pots topped with wicker lampshades stand on original grain mortars, carved from the trunk of a hardwood tree, at the side of the handcrafted wooden bed. Beaded Zulu 'love letters' adorn a simple cream cushion while a faux leopard-skin bedthrow gives the room the aura of Zulu royalty.

ABOVE: The dramatic dinner table is given a regal air by the high-backed cane 'thrones' topped with moulded resin antelope horns, richly upholstered cushions and suede bolsters. An elegant, sophisticated look is achieved with silver cutlery and simple white crockery.

RIGHT: Fine leather and wood combines with the vibrant colours of the kelim upholstery and brass tacks to create a warm but exotic look.

LONDOLOZI GAME RESERVE
sabi sand wildtuin
south africa

LEFT: THE MAIN CAMP
LOUNGE FEATURES A
COLLECTION OF HISTORIC
BLACK-AND-WHITE VARTY-
FAMILY PHOTOGRAPHS.

ABOVE: REAL ZEBRA
SKIN COVERS A CUSHION
ON AN OTTOMAN MADE
FROM A WEST AFRICAN
SENUFO DEATHBED.

Owned and run by the Varty family, Londolozi has earned a reputation over several decades as one of Africa's most genteel safari lodges. Built on the site of the original hunting camp, Londolozi's Main Camp pays tribute to the pioneers of this remarkable area. Local stone and thatch combine with majestic, living trees incorporated in the building designs to create a graceful tree-house impression where the focus is on mixing the natural with the elegant. Decor throughout the various lodges is an eclectic mix of traditional, tribal, historic and nostalgic memorabilia, all inspired by the natural world. Modern surfaces and fabrics blend with earthy and authentic finishes to create an essence that is both African and cosmopolitan, where guests can unwind after a day in the wilds.

ABOVE: A WOVEN SILK HERRINGBONE-DESIGN BEDSPREAD OFFERS A MUTED CONTRAST TO THE MUSLIN MOSQUITO

NETTING OFFSET BY MIDNIGHT PURPLE WALLS BEHIND THE BED. THE BEDSIDE LAMPS WERE MADE FROM SEGMENTS

OF A ZANZIBARI DOORPOST MOUNTED ON A WROUGHT-IRON FRAME; THE SHADES ARE BLANKET-STITCHED.

OPPOSITE TOP LEFT: A STANDARD BATHTUB SET INTO A MOULDED CEMENT PLINTH AND OCHRE-TINTED CEMENT

FLOORS INSET WITH RIVER-WORN PEBBLES.

OPPOSITE TOP RIGHT: THE SIMPLICITY OF THE SURROUNDING BUSHVELD IS MIRRORED BY THE PLAIN WHITE

WASHBASINS SET INTO AN UNTREATED CEMENT SLAB AND HANDCARVED WOODEN MIRROR FRAME.

ABOVE LEFT: A WICKER BUTLER'S TRAY FROM MALAWI AND AN OTTOMAN

COVERED IN ZEBRA SKIN GENERATE AN AURA OF SAFARI COMFORT IN THIS

SUMPTUOUS TREE LODGE BEDROOM.

ABOVE RIGHT: A LARGE WOOD-FRAMED MIRROR OVER MATCHING HIS AN

HERS PEDESTAL-MOUNTED HANDBASINS REFLECTS THE SIMPLE SPLIT-CANE

ROLLER BLINDS THAT SCREEN THE BATHROOM FROM THE EXTERIOR.

GARONGA SAFARI CAMP
makalali conservancy
south africa

LEFT: BE INDULGED BY
THE LUXURY OF A PIPING
HOT BUBBLEBATH UNDER
THE STARLIT SKIES.

ABOVE: A CALABASH
SUITCASE FROM THE IVORY
COAST POISED ON A PLINTH
INSIDE A BEDROOM DOOR.

Rough plastered curved sienna walls and columns combined with natural canvas give Garonga Safari Camp a unique and soothing feeling, inspired by the design and textures of nature's termite mounds married with Mexican adobe-style architecture. A former British Army officer, owner Bernardo Smith's holistic philosophy is to offer a unique re-earthing safari experience incorporating the sensitive beauty of the bush and encapsulating the feelings of the surroundings of his lodge. Garonga's gentle but exquisite decor is both perceptive of the camp's setting and calming to the soul, creating a strikingly elegant yet warm and tactile atmosphere. The camp is a sanctuary of tranquillity and conviviality that rejects the rigidity of modern life to recreate the natural flows of Africa's wide open spaces.

LEFT: A HANDWOVEN SILK-AND-COTTON BLEND BEDSPREAD IS FRAMED BY A CREAM MUSLIN MOSQUITO NET SUSPENDED FROM A COPPER FRAME.

TOP: THE COMBINATION OF NATURAL CANVAS AND ADOBE CONSTRUCTION CREATES A UNIQUE CHARACTER.

ABOVE: HANDWOVEN CREAM COTTON HAMMOCKS ON THE VERANDAHS VIE WITH THE HANDCRAFTED STEAMED WATTLE CHAIRS FOR A PLACE TO WHILE AWAY THE SIESTA HOURS.

ABOVE: THREE DIFFERENT METALS WERE HANDCUT AND HANDWORKED BY JOHANNESBURG

CRAFTSWOMAN SUE JOWELL TO CREATE A SUCCESSFUL MIX OF COLOURS AND PATTERNS ON THE

INTIMATE DINING TABLES.

RIGHT: A QUIET CORNER UNDER THE TREES MAKES A PEACEFUL SETTING IN WHICH TO ENJOY A

BOTTLE OF FINE WINE, READ A GOOD BOOK, OR SIMPLY FIND INSPIRATION IN NATURE.

TOP: THE LOUNGE IS AN ORGANIC, FLOWING SPACE OF PEACE AND TRANQUILLITY.

LEFT: A RECYCLED-METAL HIPPO TABLE FEATURES IN AN ALCOVE FURNISHED WITH A BUILT-IN SEAT CARRYING AN ASSORTMENT OF WOVEN AND APPLIQUED RAFFIA KUBA CLOTH CUSHIONS.

RIGHT: A LARGE CLAY BEER POT IS AN EYE-CATCHING ELEMENT IN ONE OF THE BEDROOMS.

TOP: IN HAMBLEDEN SUITE, A HANDBEATEN COPPER TUB HAS A VIEW OVER THE BUSHVELD.

LEFT: CUSTOM-MADE CERAMIC WASHSTANDS COMPLEMENT THE MINIMALIST BATHROOM DESIGN.

RIGHT: THE COPPER THEME IS FOLLOWED THROUGH IN THE INTIMATE HAMBLEDEN SUITE.

SEKALA GAME LODGE
welgevonden reserve
south africa

Bushveld hues, roughly hewn gumpoles, tawny thatched rooftops, authentic artifacts, animal prints and African fabrics combine at Sekala to recreate classic safari style. Rising out of unspoilt bushveld in the private Welgevonden Reserve in the Waterberg region of South Africa's Northern Province, Sekala's rustic tones and materials set the scene and produce a sense of balance and harmony that belies its proximity to the frenetic pace of Johannesburg, less than three hours' drive away. With a stunning view that seems to stretch forever, bathrooms that open to the wilds and a viewing deck overlooking a busy water-hole, Sekala's priority as a game-viewing destination is clear. Added to this is a high level of service and bushveld *haute cuisine* served in the open-air boma under the star-filled skies.

Natural light and soothing tones promise a restful stay. The decor combines natural stone floors, solid wood furnishings, zebra-print cushions and chair coverings. The original African artworks from West Africa are displayed to best advantage on a plain cream-painted wall.

ABOVE LEFT: A CARVED LEADWOOD LOG FROM ZIMBABWE MAKES AN INTERESTING TABLE CENTREPIECE

ON THE SLEEPER-WOOD DINING TABLE. THE ANIMAL-PRINT PLACEMATS ARE AN UNUSUAL COMBINATION

WITH THE COPPER CANDELABRA AND SILVER CUTLERY; THE MUDCLOTH ON THE DRESSER IS FROM MALI.

ABOVE RIGHT: TEXTILES, WITH THEIR CONTRASTING WEAVES AND INNOVATIVE DESIGNS, OFFER A

VALUABLE MEANS OF INTRODUCING BOTH PRACTICAL AND ATTRACTIVE TEXTURES TO A ROOM.

MAKWETI SAFARI LODGE

LEFT: BABELIKE STOOLS,

WHICH ARE HOLLOWED

AND HANDCARVED LOGS FROM

GABON, MAKE INTERESTING

INFORMAL TABLES

IN THE LOUNGE.

ABOVE: COLOURFUL

TABLEWARE ADDS VIBRANCY

TO THE BRUNCH TABLE.

Makweti, built into the craggy rock formations of the Waterberg, is a dramatic architectural synthesis of the charm and sophistication of Africa. Traditional African art melds with natural building materials, while the elegance of a bygone era is combined with the conveniences of today to create a sensual retreat. Rich colours blend with raw textures, animal hide with solid wood, and natural fibres with modern fabrics in a pleasing juxtaposition of old and new, natural and artificial. Situated in Big Five game country, the lodge has spectacular views over the pristine bushveld and rugged Waterberg Mountains. Reflecting the harmonious balance of its decor, Makweti's cuisine is an artful fusion of both local and exotic served in the elegant formal diningroom or beside a flickering campfire in the open boma.

ABOVE: A LIBERAL FUSION OF ARTWORK AND ARTIFACTS, FABRICS AND FINISHES MERGE THROUGHOUT THE ROOMS

OF THE LODGE.

RIGHT: SWATHES OF MOSQUITO NETTING AND COLOURFUL THROWS ARE COMPLEMENTED BY THE GEOMETRIC DESIGN

OF THE BEDSPREAD AND HANDCARVED KOTA FIGURINE LAMP BASES.

MKUZE FALLS GAME LODGE

kwazulu-natal
south africa

LEFT: THE CHALETS ARE BUILT
ON RAISED WOODEN DECKS
OVERLOOKING THE CROC- AND
HIPPO-FILLED RIVER.

ABOVE: BREAKFAST ON THE
HONEYMOON SUITE DECK IS
QUITE AN OCCASION.

Indigenous woods and local slate, stone, reeds and thatch make up the basis of Mkuze Falls' design features, complemented by sumptuous fabrics, original artworks and carvings from across the African continent. Mkuze Falls Game Lodge comprises eight chalets plus a honeymoon suite – each one is raised on teak decking and overlooks a tumbling waterfall on the perennial Mkuze River. The interior textures and tones combine to create a mellow comfort zone, while the large expanses of glass integrate the indoors and outdoors. Mkuze Falls is one of only two private game reserves in this province home to Africa's Big Five – lion, leopard, elephant, rhinoceros and buffalo – as well as a variety of other species.

Locally carved wooden giraffes form a focal point in the spacious lounge, which features a combination of stone, thatch and reed-clad walls.

THE USE OF GENUINE IVORY IS SOCIALLY UNACCEPTABLE NOWADAYS, BUT THESE MOULDED FIBREGLASS TUSKS LEND

A NOBLE AIR TO THE ELABORATE ELEPHANT-HIDE HEADBOARD FRAMING THESE BEDS.

PHINDA PRIVATE GAME RESERVE

conservation corporation africa
kwazulu-natal • south africa

LEFT: SOFT LIGHT FALLS
FROM UNUSUAL MEXICAN
STARLIGHTS AND THE SIMPLE
IRON CANDELABRA OVER
ROCK LODGE'S DINNER TABLE.

ABOVE: A MODERN MIX
OF CONTEMPORARY AND
TRADITIONAL ELEMENTS.

Cradled between the arms of the Ubombo Mountains in the west and the azure sweep of the Indian Ocean to the east, Phinda is located in Zululand, one of Africa's most ecologically diverse regions. Part of the Conservation Corporation Africa collection of prestige private safari lodges, Phinda has earned worldwide repute for its extraordinary biodiversity as well as its lavish and sophisticated accommodation. Each of the four distinctive lodges has its own individual flavour in style and decor, ranging from the roughly hewn stone and adobe walls and ethnic mood of Rock Lodge, the Afro-Asian motif of Vlei Lodge to the Zulu-Zen minimalist feel of Forest Lodge, where the walls have become windows opening up to the forest floor and towering torchwood trees beyond.

GLASS WALLS ALLOW THIS ROOM TO 'FLOAT' IN ITS FORESTED SURROUNDINGS. SIMPLE CANVAS BLINDS CAN BE LOWERED AT NIGHT TO ENSURE PRIVACY AND SECLUSION IN THE ROMANTIC INTERIOR. OUTSIDE, THE FOREST IS ALIVE WITH CREATURES, FROM TINY ANTELOPE TO COLOURFUL BIRDS AND RARE RED SQUIRRELS.

IN THIS FOREST LODGE BEDROOM, THE 'WINDOWS' ARE IN FACT FLOOR-TO-CEILING SLIDING-GLASS 'WINDOW-WALLS'. PALE

BLONDE BEECHWOOD FLOORING BLENDS WITH THE WOODWORK OF THE CONTEMPORARY DOUBLE BED AND MORRIS CHAIR;

THE BEDSPREAD IS A SOFT PSEUDO-SUEDE.

LEFT: A SHEET-METAL HEADBOARD WITH DESIGNS

HANDCUT USING A PLASMA CUTTER IS A MODERN FOIL

TO THE ROUGH PLASTERED ADOBE WALLS, TIMBER

ROOF TRUSSES, CEMENT FLOOR AND WOVEN CARPET.

ABOVE: NATURAL LIGHT POURS IN THROUGH HUGE

WOOD-FRAMED SLIDING WINDOWS, ENHANCING THE

RICHNESS OF THE SUMPTUOUSLY UPHOLSTERED

MORRIS CHAIR CUSHIONS IN THIS ROCK LODGE ROOM.

THIS ELEGANT TABLE SETTING IN THE VLEI LODGE DININGROOM INCLUDES RECYCLED GLASS UNDERPLATES

AND WINE GLASSES FROM SWAZILAND'S NGWENYA GLASS.

CLOCKWISE FROM TOP LEFT: A SENUFO HEADREST FROM THE IVORY COAST MAKES AN ORIGINAL VANITY STOOL. THE MONOCHROME PATTERNS OF KASAI RAFFIA VELVET FROM THE CONGO IMPART PLEASING TEXTURAL INTEREST. THE LIMEWASHED FRAME OF THIS CUPBOARD OFFSETS THE RAW FINISH OF THE SALIGNA SAPLING LATHS. ROUGH TREE-TRUNK UPRIGHTS FUSE WITH OTHER NATURAL ELEMENTS FOR AN AUTHENTIC AFRICAN LOOK. A CUT-METAL OCCASIONAL TABLE IMITATES THE FORM AND LINES OF A ZEBRA. WOOD BEAMS AND SUPPORTS USED THROUGHOUT THE LODGE APPEAL TO THE SENSES, CAPTURE ATTENTION AND DELIGHT THE EYE.

SHAMWARI LODGE

shamwari game reserve, south africa

LEFT: THE LEVEL OF
LUXURY LONGED FOR BY THE
1860 BRITISH SETTLERS.

ABOVE: THE SOFT PINK WALLS
OF LONG LEE MANOR, SET IN
THE HEART OF THE RESERVE,
ECHO THE AUTHENTICITY OF
THE MID-19TH-CENTURY
FURNISHINGS WITHIN.

Shamwari Game Reserve, which means 'my friend' in Shona, offers a gracious welcome that certainly lives up to its name. This luxury 'settlement' of five lodges delivers the perfect Eastern Cape combination of today's comforts – air-conditioning, under-floor heating and personal chefs and game rangers – and frontier-style history and heritage. The period-furnished Eagle's Cragg Lodge, Highfield and Bushman's River Lodge all date back to the days of the entrepid British Settlers of 1860, who left their lush, green homeland for the dusty open spaces of the Cape frontier. Long Lee Manor is a fully restored Edwardian Mansion, with a bewitching riverside lapa overlooking the hippo pool, while the fragrant thatch and modern ethnic decor of Lobengula Lodge provide the best in 21st-century 'rustic chic'.

ABOVE: WOOD REFLECTS CHARACTER AND WARMTH IN THIS BEDROOM WHERE A HEAVY FOUR-POSTER BED COMBINES WITH THE DOMINANT DARK PANELLING OF THE WARDROBES AND AN OLD WOODEN CHEST.

OPPOSITE TOP: A COLLECTION OF AFRICAN MASKS AND FETISHES SETS THE SCENE BUT UNDERSCORES THE SIMPLICITY OF THIS WARM AND COSY INFORMAL LOUNGE.

OPPOSITE BOTTOM: A PLAIN, LIMEWASHED WICKER BASKET FILLED WITH OSTRICH EGGS MAKES A DECORATIVE STATEMENT IN THIS FIRESIDE SETTING ON THE LOBENGULA VERANDAH. THE BOLD USE OF RICH OCHRE-PAINTED WALLS AND FABRICS WITH STRONG WEAVES AND DESIGNS ADDS TO THE CHEERFUL AND RELAXING AMBIENCE AND STRONG COUNTRY FEELING.

SOSSUSVLEI · ONGAVA · SKELETON COAST

wilderness safaris
namibia

ABOVE: SOSSUSVLEI

WILDERNESS CAMP

PERCHES ATOP A ROCKY

OUTCROP, SURROUNDED BY A

NATURAL SETTING THAT NEEDS

NO EMBELLISHMENT.

LEFT: SUNSET COLOURS

REFLECT FROM THE POOL.

Namibia's natural environment is so visually stimulating that any attempt to compete with it would be bound to fail. Keeping this firmly in mind, the Wilderness Safaris camps and lodges in Sossusvlei, Ongava and the Skeleton Coast have kept to unobtrusive and uncluttered designs. The simplicity of raw materials and natural textures keeps the rhythms of the natural environment flowing through the lodges, while a fusion of contemporary and traditional safari elements delight the eye without detracting from the views beyond. Combinations of vibrant earth tones and raw materials such as canvas and wood, stone and thatch blend in an essential wilderness mix to keep a sense of the old safaris, transcending the ephemeral nature of modern decor fashions to harmonise with the natural world.

ABOVE: TRADITIONAL SAFARI-STYLE CANVAS DIRECTOR'S CHAIRS ALONGSIDE THE ELEGANT ZAMBEZI TEAK DINING TABLE. WITH SUCH A VIEW, LITTLE EXTRA IS NEEDED BY WAY OF DECOR.

OPPOSITE TOP: A WOOD AND WROUGHT-IRON SIDE TABLE PLACED AGAINST A HUGE BOULDER (INCLUDED IN THE CONSTRUCTION OF THE MAIN LODGE) MAKES AN INFORMAL FEATURE BESIDE THE DOORWAY.

OPPOSITE BOTTOM: AN ECLECTIC COLLECTION OF OSTRICH EGGS, METAL FIGURINES, WEATHERED TWIGS AND DRIED GRASS CREATES A FOCAL POINT IN THE AIRY AND SPACIOUS LOUNGE OF SOSSUSVLEI WILDERNESS CAMP.

AN INDIGO-DYED WEST AFRICAN MOSSI CLOTH BEDSPREAD COMPLEMENTS THE TEAK-AND-RATTAN HEADBOARD, ITS SIMPLE LIZARD DESIGN ECHOING THE FAUNA OF THE SURROUNDINGS.

Simple and uncluttered, this bedroom with a spectacular view is an
oasis of quietness and inspiration.
The heavy drapes keep out both the
desert heat and cold.

Screen doors open wide to allow access to the natural world from this intimate Ongava Lodge bedroom. The cream bull-denim quilt provides a soft counterpoint to the dark stone floors and timbered walls.

ABOVE LEFT: WOVEN GRASS BASKETS COMBINE WITH WICKER CHAIRS AND TABLES IN A FUSION OF NATURAL TEXTURES.

ABOVE RIGHT: SALIGNA SAPLINGS MAKE A SENSIBLE SHADE ROOF OVER THIS SECLUDED VIEWING DECK.

TOP: AN OLD WINE BARREL MAKES AN UNUSUAL

BASE FOR A WASHBASIN IN SKELETON COAST CAMP.

LEFT: A TWISTED AND GNARLED TREE TRUNK IS A

FEATURE OF THIS BAR COUNTER.

RIGHT: THE DUNES OF SOSSUSVLEI PROMISE

A PICTURESQUE SETTING FOR A LATE-MORNING

CHAMPAGNE BRUNCH.

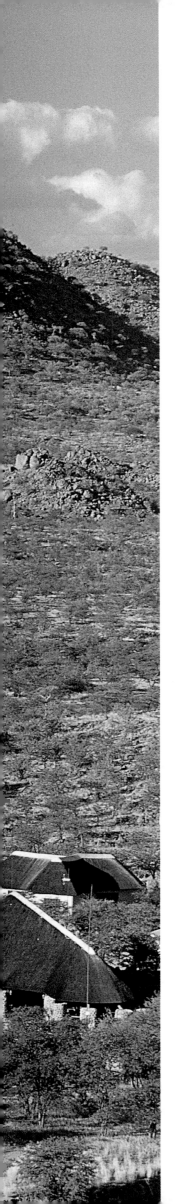

HUAB LODGE

huab conservancy
damaraland, namibia

LEFT: THE STONE AND
THATCH LODGE IS DWARFED
BY THE VASTNESS OF ITS
SURROUNDINGS.

ABOVE: STEEL CRANE SCULP-
TURES AND A PAINTED GECKO
MOTIF INSIDE THE POOL.

Damaraland is a particularly splendid region in a particularly stunning country, and in designing Huab Lodge architect Neil Hayes-Hill set out to produce something that combined rather than competed with the environment. The flowing lines of the thatch rooftops and the use of natural stone and timber wherever possible have resulted in a holistic, functional and unobtrusive design. Simple, uncluttered interiors invite relaxation within the setting of uninterrupted views of the wide open spaces surrounding the lodge. An African tenor is generated by the exposed thatch and rough poles, stone flooring and ethnic hues, while the open-plan structure of the main lodge in the Huab Conservancy, with its easy flow from indoor to outdoor, allows a sensation of belonging to the best parts of nature.

THE CLEAN LINES OF COLONIAL-STYLE TIMBER CHAIRS CLUSTERED INFORMALLY IN THE MAIN LODGE CREATE AN AREA

OF EASY LIVING — ENJOY A GOOD BOOK OR COLD NAMIBIAN BEER, OR SIMPLY WHILE AWAY THE HOURS AND WATCH

THE BIRDLIFE AT THE ROCKPOOL BELOW.

SERENE WHITE WALLS, ORGANIC STONE FLOORS AND THE RAW WOOD AND THATCH ARE A SIMPLE COUNTERPOINT TO THE VIBRANT COLOURS AND ETHNIC DESIGNS OF THE BEDSPREAD AND WATERCOLOURS BY LOCAL ARTIST JUNE OWEN-SMITH.

ENINGU CLAYHOUSE LODGE

eningu conservancy
dordabis, namibia

LEFT AND ABOVE: THE COOL

ADOBE BUILDING STYLE IS

IDEAL FOR THE EXTREMES OF

TEMPERATURE EXPERIENCED

IN THE KALAHARI, WHERE

SUMMER TEMPERATURES CAN

RISE TO SWELTERING HIGHS.

The uniquely styled clay buildings of the Eningu Clayhouse Lodge blend with the russet-coloured Kalahari sands of their surroundings. Built of 120 000 handmade clay bricks – the clay was dug and formed on the property – and creatively decorated by owners Volker and Stefanie Hümmer, the architectural design was influenced by a multitude of adobe building styles from North Africa, Greece, Mexico and Santa Fe. While the exterior reflects the hard work and enterprise of its builders, the interior is a showcase for the artistic abilities of Stefanie and her parents, carpet-weaving father Volker and mother Dörte Berner, a well-known Namibian sculptor. Unusual artworks and sculptures abound, floors are clad in handwoven Karakul wool rugs featuring ethnic designs, or painted with intriguing *trompe l'œil* carpets.

ABOVE: VIBRANT KALAHARI TONES, RICH TEXTURES AND RAW MATERIALS HELP FUSE THE SIMPLE DESIGN AND DECOR, BOTH INSIDE AND OUT, INTO A SENSUAL WHOLE. THROUGHOUT ENINGU THE FEELING IS CLEAN AND UNCLUTTERED.

RIGHT: SIMPLE BUILT-IN BEDS AND A WARDROBE FOUND IN A SECOND-HAND STORE AND RESTORED BY STEFANIE AND VOLKER ARE OFFSET BY A TROMPE L'ŒIL FLOOR AND CEILING MADE OF WATTLE FENCE DROPPERS.

LEFT: THE PANTRY DOOR WAS PAINTED WITH FARM-YARD SCENES AND COVERED WITH CHICKEN WIRE.

OPPOSITE TOP LEFT: THIS PINE CUPBOARD WAS STAINED AND DISTRESSED BY STEFANIE FOR AN AGED LOOK.

OPPOSITE TOP RIGHT: THE UNDERGROUND WINE CELLAR IS KEPT COOL WITH REGULAR DOUSINGS OF WATER FROM ABOVE.

OPPOSITE BOTTOM LEFT: AN ECLECTIC ASSORT-MENT OF AFRICAN ARTIFACTS IN THE DINING ROOM.

OPPOSITE BOTTOM RIGHT: BOLD TROMPE L'ŒIL FLOORS AND A COLOURFUL BATIK WALLHANGING BRIGHTEN THIS BEDROOM.

TONGABEZI LODGE
zambezi river
zambia

LEFT: A ROMANTIC TABLE
SET FOR TWO DRIFTS GENTLY
ATOP A MOORED SAMPAN RAFT
AS THE SUN SINKS OVER THE
ZAMBEZI RIVER.

ABOVE: THE MOST
DRAMATIC PICNIC TABLE IN
AFRICA TEETERS ON THE EDGE
OF VICTORIA FALLS.

Few rivers in Africa can compare with the Zambezi, and few lodges can better Tongabezi's incomparable setting, which encompasses peerless views over the river and faces the setting sun. Each suite, or 'house', at Tongabezi is unique – they embrace nature with their open facades yet retain a sense of intense intimacy. These romantic houses were designed with comfort uppermost in mind – we've heard the idyllic Honeymoon House described as 'worth getting married for!' Furnishings in each house are kept simple and unpretentious in order to focus attention on the scenery – this creates the impression that the rooms themselves are a part of the spectacular view. Tranquil, neutral colours are combined with untreated natural textures to complete the theme of the great African outdoors.

AN UNUSUAL FEATURE OF THIS ROOM AT TONGABEZI IS THE USE OF CONTEMPORARY AFRICAN 'COMMERCIAL ART'

ON THE WALLS. THESE ARE THE KIND OF PAINTINGS SEEN ON THE WALLS OF ROADSIDE TRADING STORES, 'SPAZA'

SHOPS AND VENDORS' STALLS, ADVERTISING TYPICAL DAY-TO-DAY COMMODITIES; THEY ARE INDEED AUTHENTIC,

MODERN AFRICAN DECOR.

TINTED AND PAINTED CONCRETE WAS USED EXTENSIVELY THROUGHOUT TONGABEZI AS A SIMPLE AND INEXPENSIVE MEANS OF FURNISHING THE LODGE. HERE, BUILT-IN BENCHES, SHELVES, ALCOVES AND THE MANTLE AROUND THE FIREPLACE IN EARTH TONES CREATE AN EASY, LIVED- IN LOOK. SCATTER CUSHIONS IN SOLID COLOURS AND ANIMAL DESIGNS ADD THE FINISHING TOUCHES.

ABOVE: BUILT SO THAT IT ALMOST TEETERS OVER THE LEGENDARY ZAMBEZI RIVER, THE BATHROOM OF THE APTLY NAMED TREE HOUSE FEATURES A SUNKEN TUB LARGE ENOUGH FOR TWO, AND A TRULY UNFORGETTABLE SETTING THAT ALLOWS A SENSE OF BEING SURROUNDED BY THE NATURAL ENVIRONMENT.

LEFT: STONE AND THATCH AND AN OVERSIZED BATHTUB IN THIS OPEN-PLAN AND OPEN-FRONTED ROOM LEND AN AIR OF ROMANCE TO ENCOURAGE GUESTS TO LIE ABED AND ENJOY THE VIEW OVER THE MAJESTIC RIVER BELOW.

ABOVE: WHEN THE LURE OF THE WATER PROVES
IRRESISTIBLE IN THE HOT AFRICAN SUN, THIS
TURQUOISE POOL OFFERS A FAR SAFER OPTION
THAN THE CROCODILE-INFESTED ZAMBEZI BEYOND.

RIGHT: A MIX OF NATURAL ELEMENTS, VIBRANT
FABRICS AND A CANOPY OF DELICATE, WHITE-
MUSLIN MOSQUITO NETTING COMBINES WITH THE
BREATHTAKING VIEW THAT CAN BE ENJOYED FROM
THE BED IN THE DREAMY TREE HOUSE SUITE.

SAUSAGE TREE CAMP

lower zambezi national park
zambia

LEFT: CAMPFIRES ARE AN

ESSENTIAL PART OF THE TRUE

AFRICAN SAFARI EXPERIENCE.

ABOVE: THE WHITE CANVAS

OF THE MESS TENT REFLECTS

A GOLDEN GLOW FROM THE

FLICKERING LAMPS.

High on the northern bank of the Zambezi River, overlooking a scenic channel dotted with lilies and home to numerous hippo, Sausage Tree Camp embodies the traditions of luxury colonial camping. Large marquee tents raised on tinted concrete platforms feature en-suite, open-air bathrooms shaded beneath towering mahogany, albida and sausage trees. After a steaming hot evening shower, taken from a canvas shower bag (filled with hot water on request), dinner is taken alfresco beneath a twinkling canopy of stars, or served by the golden light of oil lanterns in the open-sided mess tent while lions roar in the distant darkness. The Lower Zambezi National Park is one of the few true wilderness areas left in Africa, and Sausage Tree Camp recalls an era when African safaris were real-life adventures.

WOVEN BASKETS, WOOD CARVINGS,

SEEDPODS, A FEW PORCUPINE QUILLS

AND A COLLECTION OF OLD PADLOCKS

COMBINE IN AN INTERESTING DISPLAY

OF BRIC-A-BRAC THAT ADDS INTEREST

TO A CORNER OF THE LOUNGE TENT.

TINTED CEMENT IS BOTH FUNCTIONAL

AND DURABLE, THE IDEAL MATERIAL

FOR THIS OUTDOOR WASHSTAND.

ABOVE AND OVERLEAF: CREAMY NATURAL CANVAS,

SIMPLE WHITE BEDLINEN AND THE SOFT SWATHES OF

MATCHING MOSQUITO NETTING SHROUDING THE BEDS

CREATE AN AURA REMINISCENT OF SAFARIS OF OLD,

WHICH IS ENHANCED BY THE MARQUEE STYLE OF THE

TENT AND THE USE OF TRADITIONAL PARAFFIN LANTERNS.

BIG CAVE CAMP

LEFT: SUNDOWNERS AT BIG CAVE ARE SERVED ON TOP OF A MASSIVE BOULDER OVERLOOKING THE ANCIENT LANDSCAPE.

ABOVE: A ROCK ELEPHANT-SHREW WARMS ITSELF IN THE MORNING SUN.

Reposing atop a colossal granite whaleback boulder, Big Cave Camp commands inspirational views across Zimbabwe's spectacular Matobo Hills. Designed by owners Dave and Caron Waddy and built using rock, timber and thatch, nature dominates the architecture to such an extent that trees reach unfettered through the roof, giant boulders form integral parts of the internal walls and inquisitive shrews and hyrax brazenly sun themselves on the private balconies. Each luxuriously appointed thatched bungalow incorporates items reflecting the creative flair of the indigenous peoples as well as the colonial past of the country. Carefully restored period furniture mingles easily with modern and traditional African fabrics, local Ndebele clay pots and wood carvings.

GOLDEN THATCH AND THE HUES OF THE BEDSPREAD AND CUSHIONS REPRODUCE THE COLOURS OF THE SURROUNDING COUNTRYSIDE. HANDCRAFTED CLAY POTS FROM THE NEARBY GWAAI RIVER FRAME THE STAIRWAY LEADING TO THE EN-SUITE BATHROOM, AND THE BARE STONE WALLS ARE MADE FROM LOCALLY HEWN GRANITE.

Nature dominates throughout Big Cave, whether in its inclusion as part of the architecture or more simply as an essential component of the decor, such as in the handshaped, textured clay pots, left, or in the pigments derived from mud, leaves and bark in the handwoven Mali mudcloth wall-hanging and cushion covers.

LEFT: EAGLES SWOOP AND SOAR AMONG THE GIANT GRANITE BOULDERS THAT DWARF BIG CAVE CAMP. CONSTRUCTED ENTIRELY OF LOCAL MATERIALS, THE LODGE BLENDS PERFECTLY WITH THE SURROUNDING COUNTRYSIDE.

ABOVE: TEA IS SERVED IN A RELAXING CORNER OF THE PATIO, WITH SWEEPING VIEWS OF THE COUNTRYSIDE. THE ANTIQUE BEECHWOOD-AND-RATTAN SUITE, UPHOLSTERED IN LEATHER, HAS BEEN LOVINGLY RESTORED, WHILE THE SOLID TEAK TEA TABLE WAS LOCALLY SOURCED.

JAO AND KWETSANI CAMPS

ngamiland adventure safaris
okavango delta, botswana

LEFT: JAO'S FIREPLACE IS A SOCIAL FOCAL POINT, A PLACE AT WHICH TO RETELL THE DAY'S EXPERIENCES.

ABOVE: EACH ROOM AT JAO CAMP HAS ITS OWN PRIVATE 'SALA' (GAZEBO) ALONGSIDE.

Shaggy thatching, rustic timber structural details, intricately carved rosewood and saligna floors, canvas wall wraps and romantic open-air 'salas' give Jao Camp, conceived by owners David and Cathy Kays along the classic lines of a Balinese long-house, an exotic flavour. Located in one of the most beautiful areas in the heart of Botswana's Okavango Delta, both Jao and its smaller sister camp Kwetsani (built in more contemporary style using natural materials and local crafts) have been designed to offer an unrivalled safari experience, blending the best of old colonial Africa with Indonesian influences. Both camps are raised on stilted wooden decks amid ancient ebony trees and groves of wild date palms, and afford uninterrupted views over the surrounding floodplains.

ABOVE: ALL THE WOOD POLES AND BEAMS WERE SHARPENED AT THE ENDS TO LOOK LIKE STAKES,
THEN NOTCHED AND CROSSED RATHER THAN BOLTED TOGETHER.

OPPOSITE TOP LEFT: A RUSTIC DAY BED AND HANDCARVED WOODEN GONGS PROVIDE A POINT OF
INTEREST IN A CORNER OF THE SPECTACULAR DOUBLE-STOREY LOUNGE AND DININGROOM.

OPPOSITE TOP RIGHT: AFRICAN AND INDONESIAN INFLUENCES BLEND TO GIVE THE MAIN LODGE
STRUCTURE AN AIRY LIGHTNESS. EXCEPT FOR A FEW POLES HARVESTED FROM DEAD TREES, ALL
THE TIMBER USED IN THE CONSTRUCTION WAS COMMERCIALLY GROWN.

OPPOSITE BOTTOM LEFT: EARTHEN COLUMNS SUPPORTING THE LOOKOUT PLATFORM WERE INSPIRED
BY THE NATURAL FORM OF THE OKAVANGO'S EVER-PRESENT TERMITE MOUNDS.

OPPOSITE BOTTOM RIGHT: THE ELEGANT SOLID-WOOD DINING TABLE WAS HANDCRAFTED ON SITE,
USING AFRICAN ROSEWOOD IMPORTED FROM ZIMBABWE.

ABOVE LEFT: AN INVITING, FREESTANDING BALL-
AND-CLAW BATHTUB WITH MATCHING HIS-AND-HERS
CERAMIC WASHBASINS.

ABOVE RIGHT: THE AIRY BEDROOMS ARE FRONTED
BY WOOD-AND-GAUZE CONCERTINA DOORS THAT
OPEN TO THE BROAD, SHADED DECK. WOODEN
DOWELS AND STUDS RATHER THAN NAILS AND
SCREWS HOLD THE WOODWORK TOGETHER.

THE SPACIOUS CANVAS-WALLED CHALET-STYLE TENTS
FEATURE PANELLED SALIGNA FLOORS WITH INTRICATE
CARVED DETAIL. ALL THE WOODWORK, INCLUDING
THE CONSTRUCTION OF THE BED, HEADBOARD AND
DIVIDER, WAS DONE ON SITE. THE LARGE, CENTRAL
BED IS COVERED WITH AN INDIAN COTTON BED-
SPREAD AND FRAMED BY SOFTLY DRAPING MOSQUITO
NETTING. THE GAUZY CANOPY INCORPORATES AN
OVERHEAD FAN.

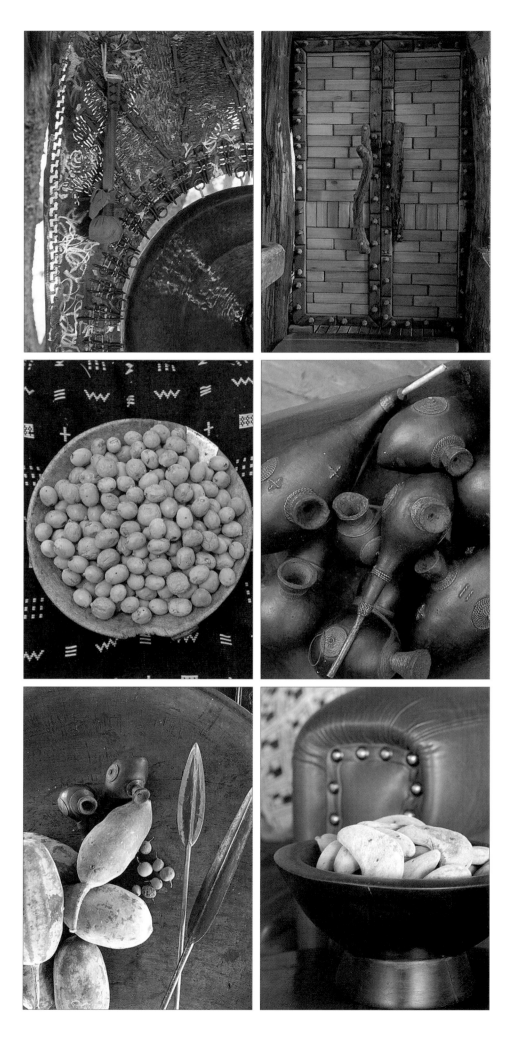

A COMBINATION OF NATURAL
AND ARTIFICIAL ARTIFACTS, WILD
FRUITS AND SEEDPODS GIVE
BOTH JAO AND KWETSANI
CAMPS THEIR UNIQUE AFRO-
INDONESIAN FLAVOUR. THE
RICH, WARM TEXTURES OF WORN
LEATHER FURNISHINGS, WOVEN
AFRICAN FABRICS IN NATURAL
DYES AND WOOD PANELLING
CONTRASTS WITH THE BEATEN
AND CUT-STEEL DINNER GONG
AND THE COLD STEEL OF
TRIBAL SPEARS.

THE LOUNGE AT KWETSANI CAMP IS FURNISHED AND DECORATED IN A CONTEMPORARY STYLE, COMBINING COMFORTABLE ARMCHAIRS AND PLUSH LEATHER COUCHES WITH CARVED AFRICAN SIDE-TABLES AND AN OTTOMAN COVERED WITH A BOLD WOVEN FABRIC. FIBRE MATTING MAKES A DURABLE COVERING FOR THE TIMBER FLOOR. THE BASKET IN THE FOREGROUND IS AN EXAMPLE OF LOCAL BOTSWANA CRAFT.

LEFT: WALLS AND DOORS CONSTRUCTED OF SAPLING FENCE DROPPERS INTRODUCE A RUSTIC COMPLEXION TO THE CAMPS. THE SIMPLE, EFFECTIVE MOSQUITO GAUZE WINDOWS CAN BE CLOSED BY LOWERING GRASS MAT ROLLER BLINDS IN THIS COSY BEDROOM.

ABOVE: KWETSANI'S ROMANTIC CANVAS, WOOD AND THATCH TREE-HOUSE CHALETS OFFER SPLENDID VIEWS AND SUPERB BIRDING OPPORTUNITIES WITHOUT THE NEED TO EVEN GET OUT OF BED!

TOP: THE AFRICAN JACANA, OR LILY-TROTTER, IS JUST ONE OF MORE THAN 350 BIRD SPECIES THAT CALL THE OKAVANGO DELTA HOME.

JACK'S AND SAN CAMPS

uncharted africa safaris
makgadikgadi pans, botswana

LEFT AND ABOVE: SAN
CAMP'S UNIQUE, DESOLATE
SETTING AND STARK WHITE
CANVAS CONJURE UP IMAGES
OF THE ROMANTIC STORY OF
'LAWRENCE OF ARABIA'.

Set among glades of towering palms on the edge of the desolate Makgadikgadi Pans in Botswana's Kalahari heartland, Jack's and San camps invoke a sense of the old, uncharted Africa. Classically proportioned safari tents are positioned for maximum privacy and perfect views; each one features its own private, open-air bathroom with shower bags — hand-filled on demand with water of the preferred temperature — suspended from the trees. Traditional wood and canvas safari accoutrements dating back to the Twenties relive the safaris of yore, with time-worn Persian rugs and dhurries scattered abundantly throughout. Damask tablecloths and bone-handled china adorn the tables, while copper and brass add a warm patina to the innovative design.

Towering makalane palms sway seductively in the breeze above the large marquee-style 'mess' tent housing San Camp's lounge and dining room. The white canvas is both functional and beautiful: it imparts a gracious air as well as helping to reflect and dispel the hot Kalahari sun.

THE EVENING COCKTAIL TABLE AWAITS THE ARRIVAL OF GUESTS AFTER THE AFTERNOON 'QUAD-BIKE' RIDE OVER

THE ENDLESS EXPANSE OF THE MAKGADIKGADI PANS' SALT FLATS. IN TIMES OF GOOD RAINS THESE PANS CAN

FILL WITH A SHALLOW EXPANSE OF WATER, ATTRACTING HUGE FLOCKS OF FLAMINGOES AND OTHER BIRDS.

CLOCKWISE FROM TOP LEFT: A BROWN HYENA CROSSES A DRIED AND CRACKED SALT PAN. JACK'S CAMP FEATURES CLASSIC COLONIAL DECOR AND ACCOUTREMENTS. THE MEERCAT, OR SURICATE, IS A CUTE AND FASCINATING INHABITANT OF THE SURROUNDING KALAHARI GRASSLANDS.

THE PERSIAN RUGS AND DHURRIES ON THE FLOOR OF

THIS TRADITIONAL SAFARI TENT ADD A PLUSH ELEMENT

NOT NECESSARILY PART OF ALL THOSE SAFARI EXPEDI-

TIONS A CENTURY OR SO AGO. THE HEAVY WOODEN

CHESTS FEATURE BRASS CORNER PIECES AND THE SIMPLE

DUVET COVER IS MADE FROM MATTRESS TICKING.

ABU CAMP
elephant back safaris
okavango delta, botswana

LEFT: Up close and

personal — one of the

elephants at Abu Camp.

ABOVE: The highly

structured architect-

designed tents were

inspired by the lines of

the Sydney Opera House.

Concealed in a picturesque riverine forest, Abu Camp redefines tented safari elegance. The tents were designed by an architect, inspired by Sydney's famous opera house and the classic lines of Bedouin tents. Each one is lavishly furnished without being ostentatious; with an eclectic selection of form, texture and colour, the decor's strength lies in the way in which diverse elements have been mixed and matched to recreate a sense of the grandest days of colonial splendour. Owner Randall J Moore is a self-confessed 'impulse buyer', and the bric-a-brac and ornaments adorning the shelves and tables is testament to this truth. The artful juxtaposition of sumptuous fabrics, worn leather, classic furnishings and individually framed photographs creates a harmonious whole.

A TERRY MATTHEWS BRONZE CAST OF CAMP NAMESAKE,

THE PLACID ELEPHANT BULL ABU, AND A 2 000-PAGE

HANDMADE LEATHER JOURNAL FROM SRI LANKA ADORN

AN OCCASIONAL TABLE CREATED FROM AN ANTIQUE

INDIAN CHAPEL WINDOW. THE READING LAMPS IN THIS

COSY READING ROOM/LOUNGE WERE MADE FROM OLD

WAGON-WHEEL HUBS.

An antique Indian latrine was renovated and restored as a quaint love-seat, covered with bright handwoven fabrics from West Africa. The leather suitcase stack-cabinet is a modern replica of that old essential of the Victorian era of luxury travel. A collection of framed photographs imbue this room with a homely and informal quality.

ABOVE: SUMPTUOUS FURNISHINGS AND FABRICS, GLEAMING LOUNGERS, POLISHED TEAK FLOORS, RICHLY COLOURED KELIMS AND A PRIVATE SUNDECK OVERLOOKING A PALM-FRINGED LILY-POND ADD UP TO A SENSUAL EXPERIENCE OF ABSOLUTE LUXURY.

OPPOSITE: A CUSTOM-MADE MAHOGANY SLEIGH BED WITH A LUXURIANT SERENGETI INK LEOPARD-PRINT QUILTED BEDCOVER IS FLANKED BY NOVEL COTTON BOBBIN LAMPS WITH SEAGRASS SHADES.

OPPOSITE: SOLID BRASS AND COPPER BATHTUBS WERE IMPORTED FROM ITALY.

ABOVE: THE DRAPED MAHOGANY FOUR-POSTER BED SETS THE MOOD IN THE MAIN SUITE; THE UNUSUAL LAMP BASE IS A CONVERTED TEA CADDY.

LEFT: THE ANTIQUE BINOCULARS WERE FOUND BY RANDALL MOORE AT A STREET SALE IN PARIS.

BOTTOM: A COLLECTION OF FRAMED PHOTOGRAPHS ADORNS THE RAGGED OCHRE BATHROOM WALLS.

SHINDE ISLAND CAMP

ker and downey safaris
okavango delta, botswana

Ker and Downey is a name almost as old as the concept of safari, dating to the early days of safari travel and hunting in Kenya and the country then known as Tanganyika (now Tanzania). Shinde Island Camp is also a camp very close to our hearts, for it was here, in the mid-Eighties, that we gained our first experience in safari-lodge management and bush life. Though considerably revamped and remodelled since then, Shinde maintains an air of those early safaris, with spacious East African-style 'Meru' tents with polished teak floors, a large communal dining table and coffee around the campfire after dinner. The main lodge structure is decorated with a collection of traditional African masks and contemporary Botswana basketry combined with animal prints and modern designs.

LEFT AND ABOVE: THE UNUSUAL MAIN LODGE IS BUILT ON SEVERAL LEVELS IN THE TREES, WHERE GUESTS CAN ENJOY COOL AFTERNOON BREEZES WHILE ADMIRING THE VIEW OVER THE WATERWAYS.

The cream interiors of Shinde's original

East African-style Meru tents are a soothing

complement to the colourful bedlinen, which

features a patchwork of naive but effective

animal prints. The floors and furnishings are

a   contrasting dark wood.

A COLLECTION OF DIVERSE LOCAL BOTSWANA BASKETRY,

WOOD CARVINGS, MASKS AND FETISHES FROM CENTRAL

AND WEST AFRICA, TOGETHER WITH CONTEMPORARY

ANIMAL PRINT FABRICS, IS USED TO GIVE SHINDE'S

UNUSUAL BARREL-VAULTED MAIN STRUCTURE AN

AUTHENTIC AFRICAN FLAVOUR.

LEBALA CAMP

kwando wildlife experience
kwando, botswana

Kwando Lebala, a classic, rustic, tented safari camp incorporating spacious L-shaped tents, is built on raised teak decking in one of Botswana's wildest and most remote corners. The camp fronts the Kwando-Linyanti wetlands, while open grasslands dotted with swaying palms and inhabited by prolific numbers of predators (most notably lion, cheetah and wild dogs) stretch away to the south and west. The 16-bed camp is furnished and decorated simply yet comfortably, with Victorian ball-and-claw bathtubs, his-and-hers washbasins and an alfresco shower for those who prefer to spend as much time as possible under the African skies. Each tent has its own secluded sundeck, with views of the endless plains beyond and their large population of elephant herds and Cape buffalo.

LEFT: A COSY, SAFARI-CAMP AMBIENCE: SOLID ZAMBEZI TEAK SIDE TABLES WITH MATCHING MORRIS CHAIRS AND BENCHES UPHOLSTERED IN SAFARI-GREEN CANVAS AND ANIMAL PRINT SCATTER CUSHIONS.

TOP: EMBROIDERED COTTON BEDTHROWS ADD SOFT-NESS TO THIS SPARSELY DECORATED TENTED ROOM.

BOTTOM: GUESTS CAN LUXURIATE IN THE BALL-AND-CLAW BATHTUB OR ENJOY THE OPEN-AIR SHOWER.

MOMBO CAMP

okavango wilderness safaris
okavango delta, botswana

In designing the new Mombo Camp, the innovative team of Silvio Rech and Lesley Carstens has taken inspiration from early African architecture and borrowed from indigenous patterns and designs. This camp, although without doubt the ultimate in tented luxury, maintains a vital interaction with the natural world, and the design team has taken an elemental approach to colour and texture – there is a sense of interior drama in keeping with the Okavango Delta's extraordinary diversity of wildlife. Enormous double-tent bedrooms offer panoramic views over the floodplains, while the captivating style of the wood-and-thatch lounge and dining areas blend with the landscape. The decor is a pleasing combination of both classic and contemporary Africa.

OPPOSITE TOP, FROM LEFT TO RIGHT: A LAMPSHADE COVERED IN GUINEAFOWL FEATHERS IS A NEAT COUNTERPOINT TO

THE CARVED WOOD HEADRESTS ON THIS LIMEWASHED WRITING TABLE. SIDE-BY-SIDE TWIN INDOOR SHOWERS AND HIS-

AND-HERS CERAMIC WASHBASINS ARE SUPPLEMENTED BY A SEPARATE OUTDOOR SHOWER UNDER THE STARS.

A KUBA CLOTH TABLE RUNNER WITH COWRIE DETAIL COMPLEMENTS THE PORCUPINE QUILL LAMPSHADE.

ABOVE AND OPPOSITE BOTTOM: THE SPACIOUS BEDROOM AND BATHROOM COMPRISE TWO INTERCONNECTED

HIGH-ROOFED TENTS WITH ROUGH-HEWN GUMPOLE SUPPORTS. THE CAREFUL COMBINATION OF CLEAN LINES,

WAFFLE-WEAVE LINEN, STITCHED LEATHER AND WOOD CO-ORDINATES SIMPLICITY WITH LUXURY.

FINE PORCELAIN, SILVER TABLEWARE AND THE BEST WINES
FOLLOW IN THE ELEGANT TRADITIONS OF SAFARIS OF YORE.
THE CHUNKY CERAMIC SOUP BOWLS WERE MADE TO ORDER
BY BONNIE FRIEDMAN OF JOHANNESBURG, WHILE THE
SOLID, LAMINATED EUCALYPTUS TABLE WAS HANDCRAFTED
ON SITE. THE CANVAS AND TEAK DIRECTOR'S CHAIRS KEEP
THE LOOK 'SAFARI'.

A PALM-NUT AND STONE SCREEN ALLOWS THE GENTLE OKAVANGO BREEZES TO WAFT THROUGH THE MAIN LOUNGE, WHICH IS FURNISHED IN A MIX OF CONTEMPORARY AND RUSTIC STYLES. COFFEE TABLES MADE FROM SEAGRASS IN A HANDWOVEN BASKET-WEAVE COMPLEMENT THE RICH LEATHER COLONIAL-STYLE SOFAS ADORNED WITH WOVEN RAFFIA KASAI VELVET KUBA CUSHIONS AND FIBRE FLOOR MATTING.

A WOODEN PYGMY BED FROM THE CONGO MAKES AN INTERESTING COFFEE TABLE IN THE COSY LIBRARY ADJACENT TO MOMBO'S MAIN LOUNGE. SELECT A GOOD BOOK FROM THE GLASS-FRONTED CABINETS AND RELAX ON A TRADITIONAL GEORGE SMITH COUCH COVERED WITH BULL-DENIM SLIPCOVERS AND CHOCOLATE CHENILLE CUSHIONS, OR WRITE A POSTCARD AT ONE OF THE INFORMAL WRITING DESKS.

CHIEF'S CAMP

abercrombie & kent
okavango delta, botswana

Skilfully integrated into the landscape, Chief's Camp and its 12 individually decorated canvas suites is built under towering shade trees on the edge of a permanent floodplain on the Okavango Delta, which attracts wildlife to its waters and nutritious grazing all year round. Chief's Camp has the lightness and serenity, the subtle elegance that is the new tradition of contemporary Africa. Attention to detail throughout the camp, and high standards of personal service and cuisine, combine with the Okavango's seductive beauty to promise (and deliver) both pleasure and adventure. Blending a fuss-free mood with local character, and using light-coloured woods, seagrass and split cane wherever possible, the emphasis in on informal and relaxed outdoor living.

TOP: THE AZURE POOL OVERLOOKS THE FLOODPLAIN.

ABOVE: UNVARNISHED BLEACHED CANE FURNITURE IS PART
OF THE LOUNGE'S RELAXED AND INFORMAL APPEAL.

RIGHT: PRINTED COTTON AND KUBA CLOTH CUSHIONS
ENHANCE THE SOLID TEAK BENCH AND CHAIRS ON THE
DECK WHERE HIGH TEA IS SERVED.

MAXIMUM USE OF LIGHT WOOD, CANE AND SEAGRASS COMBINED WITH WAFFLE-WEAVE COTTON AND TRADITIONAL

AFRICAN FABRICS CREATE AN INTERIOR FULL OF TEXTURE, WHILE AN OPEN CANVAS CLOSET WITH CANE DRAWERS

EMPHASISES THE CASUAL, HOLIDAY FEELING. THE TEKE MASKS AT LEFT ARE FROM THE CAMEROON.

CAMEROONIAN TRIBAL TOTEMS ADORN THE WALL ABOVE A SLICED-CANE SOFA WITH APPLIQUED KUBA CLOTH CUSHIONS. TWIN BLEACHED-CANE OTTOMANS ARE MATCHED BY TWIN WROUGHT-IRON AND CONE-SHAPED CANE TABLE LAMPS ON THE TEAK BOOKCASE, WHICH DISPLAYS AFRICAN MASKS AND WOODEN BOWLS.

SANDIBE SAFARI LODGE
conservation corporation africa
okavango delta, botswana

LEFT: TOWERING TREES

WERE INCORPORATED IN THE

DESIGN AND CONSTRUCTION

OF THE BUILDINGS.

ABOVE: LATE AFTERNOON

SUN CASTS A WARM GLOW

OVER THE INFORMAL OPEN-

FRONTED LOUNGE AREA.

Built with a commitment to environmental sensitivity and a recognition of Okavango's magical beauty, Sandibe Safari Lodge shelters in a forest of wild palms and twisted fig trees flanked by the clear channels of the Delta's waterways. The layered thatch roofing and adobe walls harmonise with the colours, shades and textures of the surrounding woodland, while the decor within the Lodge makes extensive use of tribal artifacts and traditional fabrics. The clever combination of old and new gives the lodge its distinctive 'contemporary safari' look of simple, carefully conceived luxury. The heart of the camp is a soaring lounge and diningroom, its open-fronted mezzanine viewing deck situated within a cathedral-like grove of wild ebony, knobthorn and sycamore fig trees.

ABOVE: A RAW SILK THROW RUG AND WOVEN LEATHER BEDSPREAD IS FRAMED BY A SWATHE OF DOBBY-WEAVE MOSQUITO NETTING SUSPENDED OVER THE LARGE BED.

OPPOSITE TOP LEFT: THE CLEAN LINES OF A MODERN CHAIR BY CCA'S CHRIS BROWN CONTRASTS WITH THE ORGANIC SHAPES OF THE CENTRAL AFRICAN MASKS OVERHEAD.

OPPOSITE TOP RIGHT: THE CONE-SHAPED HANDBEATEN BRASS BEDSIDE LAMP WITH OSTRICH EGG CENTREPIECE STANDS ON A BABELIKE STOOL FROM GABON.

OPPOSITE BOTTOM LEFT: SHADED BY TOWERING TREES AND COOLED BY THE BREEZE, THE WOOD-AND-NYLON CORD HAMMOCK IS A FINE PLACE TO WAIT FOR THE MIDDAY HEAT TO SUBSIDE.

OPPOSITE BOTTOM RIGHT: OLD WOODEN BOWLS HAVE BEEN INVERTED TO SERVE AS LAMP-SHADES ABOVE THE TWIN WASHBASINS SET INTO A SOLID TIMBER COUNTER.

LEFT: THE GEOMETRIC PATTERNS OF THE MALI MUDCLOTH MAKE A BOLD STATEMENT ALONGSIDE THE PSEUDO-SUEDE OTTOMANS AND WICKER TABLE.

TOP: A CONSTELLATION OF CANDLES CASTS A HALO OF LIGHT OVER A TABLE FOR TWO.

BOTTOM: THE CONTRASTING TEXTURAL QUALITIES AND RUSTIC HUES OF RAW SILK, WEST AFRICAN BARK CLOTH AND WOVEN LEATHER.

REILLY'S ROCK
mlilwane game reserve
swaziland

LEFT: THE COOL AND
SHADY VERANDAH RUNNING
THE LENGTH OF THE HOUSE
IS THE PERFECT PLACE IN
WHICH TO RELAX.

TOP: REILLY'S ROCK IS
SET IN MAGNIFICENT SHADY
AND LAWNED GARDENS.

Set amid magnificent gardens against a backdrop of the imposing Nyonyane Mountain (Execution Rock) over-looking the scenic Ezulwini Valley, this original 'out of Africa' colonial homestead has been painstakingly restored by owners Ted and Liz Reilly. Exquisitely furnished interiors and charming bedrooms filled with genuine period pieces give the historic lodge the welcoming character of a comfortable old farmhouse. Constructed in exchange for an ox-wagon at the end of World War I, the Lodge was built of hand-hewn rock as the home of settler and tin miner James Weighton Reilly, Ted's father. Today the Lodge has a wealth of Swaziland's early pioneer history locked within its solid stone walls.

TOP: THE MAIN SUITE, OR GOGO'S ROOM, FEATURES THE ORIGINAL BED USED BY OWNER TED REILLY'S MOTHER EARLY LAST CENTURY.

CENTRE: THE FIREPLACE DOMINATES THE LOUNGE, FLANKED ON BOTH SIDES BY CABINETS MADE ON SITE FROM SLEEPER WOOD SALVAGED FROM THE OLD RAILWAY LINE.

LEFT: THE ANTIQUE BRASS BED IN THIS BEDROOM WAS PART OF THE ORIGINAL FURNITURE IN THE HOME.

TOP: THE ORIGINAL EARLY 20TH-CENTURY WASH-STAND WITH MARBLE TOP AND TILED SPLASHBACK, COMPLETE WITH CHINA WASHBOWL AND EWER, IS IN KEEPING WITH THE OVERALL COLONIAL THEME.

ABOVE: MUTED COLOURS CREATE A RESTFUL FORMAL BEDROOM.

BENGUERRA ISLAND LODGE

bazaruto archipelago
mozambique

LEFT: AS BEFITTING ITS
LOCATION, FRESH FISH AND
SEAFOOD ARE A FEATURE
OF BENGUERRA'S MENU.

ABOVE: THE CHARMING,
RUSTIC MAIN LODGE IS SET
BACK FROM THE BEACH.

Robinson Crusoe could not have asked for a more idyllic hideaway, and certainly Man Friday would have had a difficult time trying to match the levels of hands-on service and attention that have made Benguerra Lodge the desert-island refuge of the cognoscenti. Local builders and crafters were used wherever possible in the construction of the lodge, with natural building materials predominating. Reeds and palm fronds were used for the walls, and the roofs were thatched. The picturesque open-fronted bedrooms are but a shell's-throw from the ocean. The decor is a colourful mix of local screen-printed fabrics, faux bamboo furniture, indigenous basketware and seashells washed up on the endless sandy beaches.

LEFT: HISTORIC BLACK-AND-WHITE PHOTOGRAPHS DEPICTING THE

EARLY DAYS IN THIS FORMER PORTUGUESE COLONY LINE THE REED

AND PALM-FROND WALLS OF THE BAR.

RIGHT: GRASS BASKETS AND OLD PAINTED MORTARS CREATE

DECORATIVE INTEREST IN A CORNER OF THE DINING ROOM.

OPPOSITE: COLOURFUL ORIGINAL PAINTINGS AND LOCAL SCREEN-

PRINTED FABRICS CREATE AN ESSENTIAL 'ISLAND HOLIDAY' FEEL.

LEFT: A DILAPIDATED DHOW PULLED UP THE BEACH

MAKES A PERFECT SUNDOWNER SPOT.

ABOVE: THE OPEN-FRONTED BEDROOMS FACE THE

NEARBY OCEAN AND ARE DECORATED WITH SEASHELLS

AND FUNCTIONAL MOSQUITO NETTING. THE OVERHEAD

FAN IS A NECESSITY IN THE HEAT OF SUMMER NIGHT

IN THE TROPICS.

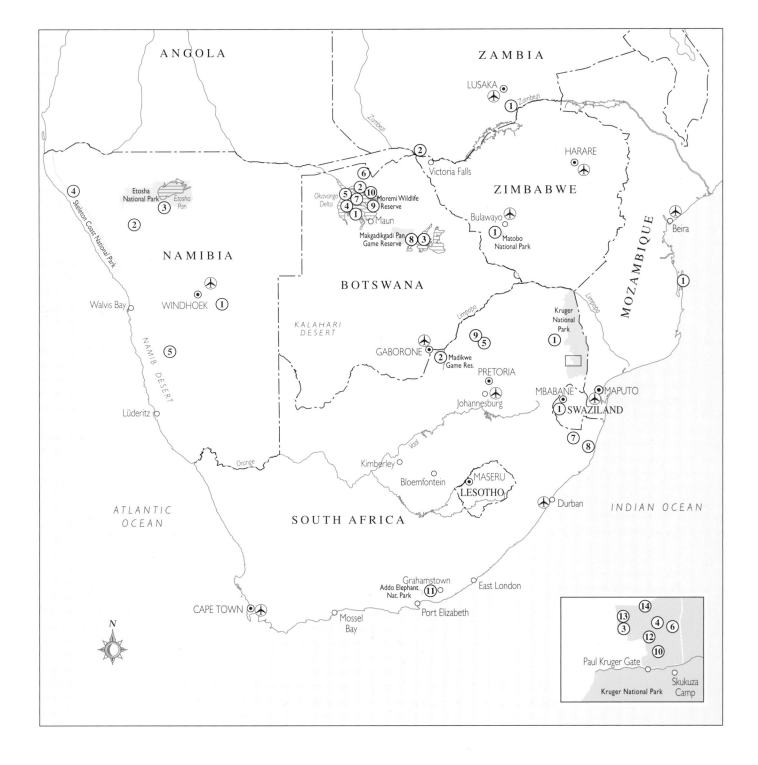

BOTSWANA

1 Abu Camp
2 Chief's Camp
3 Jack's Camp
4 Jao Camp
5 Kwetsani Camp
6 Lebala Camp
7 Mombo Camp
8 San Camp
9 Sandibe Safari Lodge
10 Shinde Island Camp

MOZAMBIQUE

1 Benguerra Island Lodge

NAMIBIA

1 Eningu Clayhouse Lodge
2 Huab Lodge
3 Ongava Lodge
4 Skeleton Coast Camp
5 Sossusvlei Wilderness Camp

SOUTH AFRICA

1 Garonga Safari Camp
2 Jaci's Safari Lodge

3 Leopard Hills Game Reserve
4 Londolozi Game Reserve
5 Makweti Safari Lodge
6 Mala Mala Game Reserve
7 Mkuze Falls Game Lodge
8 Phinda Private Game Reserve
9 Sekala Game Lodge
10 Selati Lodge: Sabi Sabi
11 Shamwari Lodge
12 Singita Private Game Reserve
13 Ulusaba Rock Lodge
14 Vuyatela: Djuma Game
     Reserve

SWAZILAND

1 Reilly's Rock

ZAMBIA

1 Sausage Tree Camp
2 Tongabezi Lodge

ZIMBABWE

1 Big Cave Camp

ACKNOWLEDGEMENTS

This book would not have come into existence without the support and co-operation of a great many people. We would like to extend our sincere thanks to everyone who has assisted in so many different ways, the owners, management and staff of all the camps and lodges featured herein, the numerous bush pilots who flew us into remote airstrips and the friends and family who have encouraged and supported us in our ventures and adventures over the years. We are also grateful for the continued assistance and support of Foto Distributors (Pty) Ltd of Johannesburg, importers of Nikon cameras and lenses, which we use exclusively in our work, Citylab (Sandton) for the care always taken in developing our films, Land Rover (South Africa), Cussons Land Rovers in Nelspruit, Sean and Wilma Beneke of Mhlume, Swaziland, and Jeffery Kempson in Johannesburg. We have always been especially grateful for the friendship and gracious hospitality of our dear friends Billy and Mich Cochrane in Johannesburg and Keith and Colleen Begg in Cape Town.

For their assistance during the visits to the camps and lodges we would like to thank Jan and Jaci van Heteren, Pieter Dros, Jim Makubela, Simon Blackburn, Bruce Little, Andrew McEwan, Ingrid Nielsen, Allan Matuda, Jonathan Lithgow, Senamile Mazibuko, Duncan and Louise Rodgers, Carmen Shelley, Hennie de Clerk, Philip Hatting, Campbell and Pendrae Scott, Liane Allaway, Tony Reumerman, Thembi Mdluli, Rory du Plessis, Michelle Collett, Bex Leigh, Martijn Brouwer, Josie Stowe, Renee Flanagan, Esther Nkosi, John Huxter, Byron Ross, Romain Sauvage, Chris Brown, Bernardo Smith, Trish Marshall, Jefferey Funk, Mickhaeal von Hagen, Mariska Grobler, Rick Lahner, Tish van Rooyen, Morné Koort, Andy Boesch, Bryan Olver, Craig and Chantan Macdonald, Barbara Roth, Mike Munro, Eric Buthelezi, Anthony Collett, Joe Cloete, Lumley Hulley,

Nikki Waterhouse, Andrew Gillies, Melissa London, Colin Bell, Dave and Jennifer van Smeerdijk, Frans due Raan, Chris Liebenberg, Michelle Kittel, Sean Patrick, Jackie Kruger, Dee Geelink, Chris Bakkes, Jan and Suzi van de Reep, Bernd and Erica Brell, Volker and Stefanie Hümmer, Ben and Vanessa Parker, Charlie Maxse, George Maduvanhu, Jason Motte, David Kys, Dave and Caron Waddy, David and Cathy Kays, Richard and Barbara Galpin, Andrew Greathead, Sally Wheatley, Grant Atkinson, Tammy Goble, Taboka Chiabe, Warren Becker, Kerry Blewett, Ralph Bousfield, Catherine Raphaely, Glyn Maude, Randall J Moore, Sandor Carter, Adrian Dandridge, Daniella Blaëtter, Hilary van der Colff, Jimmy Bontsikabae, Chris and Diana Kruger, Lloyd and Sue Camp, Mike Penman, Silvio Rech, Lesley Carstens, Mike Papenfus, Karryn Salman, Nandi Retiyo, Andre and Irene Simpson, Nation Mphela, Dougie and Diane Wright, Paul and Jill Woods, Willie Senokora, Robert Sekeseke, Ras Munduu, Coolie Setswamokwena, Oliver Madibela, Steven Stockhall, Ashleigh Harris, Judy Mosasa, Ipotseng Modinga, Ted and Liz Reilly, Patricia Dludlu, Margie Macduff, Sally Bryson, Arthur and Shelley Zeederberg.

We must also thank the team at Struik Publishers, especially project managers Linda de Villiers and, initially, Pippa Parker, Caroline Konstant – without whom our arrangements would have been a nightmare – and most specially, Petal Palmer, whose endless patience and sympathetic design means so much to how this book looks.

Last but not least we wish to record our eternal love and gratitude to our parents whose unfaltering suport and assistance over the years has meant so much to the fulfilment of our dreams.

DARYL AND SHARNA BALFOUR,
Cape Town, September 2000.

S I M P L Y
S A F A R I

For further information, reservations and bookings

check the website www.simplysafari.com for a complete on-line service

or write to Simply Safari, P O Box 781454, Sandton, 2146, South Africa.

Struik Publishers (Pty) Ltd

(a member of Struik New Holland Publishing (Pty) Ltd)

Cornelis Struik House

80 McKenzie Street

Cape Town 8001

Reg. No.: 1954/000965/07

ISBN 1 86872 532 4

First published in 2001

2 4 6 8 10 9 7 5 3 1

PUBLISHING MANAGER: Linda de Villiers

DESIGNER: Petal Palmer

DESIGN ASSISTANT: Natascha Adendorff

EDITOR: Gail Jennings

CARTOGRAPHER: John Hall

Reproduction by Hirt & Carter Cape (Pty) Ltd

Printed and bound by Kyodo Printing Co (Singapore) Pte Ltd